My First Book of
Arabic Words

Let's Learn Some Arabic!

There are 28 letters in the Arabic alphabet,
two more than the English alphabet.
As some sounds and letters don't directly correlate,
to apply the ABC format to Arabic, a few variants and
creative choices are necessary. The rhymes for
the letters C, G, H, O, P and V introduce English words
first and then their Arabic counterparts. For X,
a simple word that doesn't start with that
letter is introduced instead.
The chart on page 31 lists the
words introduced.

My First Book of Arabic Words

An ABC Rhyming Book of Arabic Language and Culture

by Aya Khalil
Illustrated by Chaymaa Sobhy

TUTTLE Publishing

Tokyo | Rutland, Vermont | Singapore

Introduction

Not every letter and sound in Arabic has a direct counterpart in English. Here's a guide to the letters and sounds you'll find in the alphabet rhymes.

Arabic Letter	Sound	Example
ء	١	uh['] oh
ب	b	bat
ت	t	sat
ث	*th*	three
ج	J	jar
ح	ḥ	--
خ	*kh*	khaled
د	d	dad
ذ	*thz*	there
ر	r	rat
ز	z	zoo
س	s	sand
ش	*sh*	ship
ص	ṣ	saw
ض	ḍ	--
ط	ṭ	--
ظ	ẓ	--
ع	ç	--

Arabic Letter	Sound	Example
غ	*gh*	--
ف	f	fat
ق	q	cool
ك	k	kit
ل	l	lion
م	m	money
ن	n	nap
ه	h	hot
و	w	wow
ي	y	yard
ـَ	a	cat
أ	aa	tab (extend the /a/ sound a little more, as if taaab)
ـُ	u	pool
وُ	uu	zoo
ـِ	i	kit
يِ	ii	sheet

Thanks to Islam Farag, University of Pittsburgh, for the use of his transliteration system.

أَهْلًا

'ahlan

A is for **'ahlan!**
Welcome, my new friend
make yourself at home,
you can have the comfy end.

5

بِطّيخ

biṭ-ṭiikh

B is for **biṭ-ṭiikh**,
Watermelon ripe and sweet
On a humid day like this
Our favorite summer treat.

سَيَّارَة

say-yaarah

C is for **car**
say-yaarah is what we say.
My mom's a safe driver
slow and steady all the way.

دَرَّاجَة

dar-raajah

D is for *dar-raajah*,
a bike that's blue and bright.
Find a friend to ride with
and pedal out of sight.

عِيدُ الْفِطْر

çiidu-lfiṭr

E is for **Eid al-fitr**,
We celebrate! We eat!
Gather at the table.
Can you find a seat?

9

فُسْتَان

fustaan

F is for *fustaan*,
A dress of softest pink.
I wear it for my birthday
what do you think?

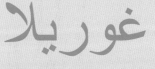

غوريلا

ghuriil-lah

G is for **gorilla**.
ghuriil-lah, beats his chest.
He spends the morning eating
then it's time for a rest.

منزل

manzil

H is for **house**
or you can say *manzil*.
So glad you're dropping by
sharing stories and a meal.

إِبْرَة

'ibrah

I is for *'ibrah*
"Look, the rip has spread!"
Dad sews up teddy's back
with a **needle** and some thread.

J is for *jubn*

I love all kinds of **cheese**.
For breakfast or a snack
Can I have some more, please?

جُبْن

jubn

كِتَاب

kitaab

K is for *kitaab*
I take my **book** everywhere
in the car or to the park
just one more page, I swear!

لَيْمُون

laymuun

L is for *laymuun*
who wants some lemonade?
It's perfect for our picnic
delicious and homemade.

مَدْرَسَة

madrasah

M is for *madrasah*
I really love my **school**.
Kindness toward others
is the number one rule.

17

نَجْم

najm

N is for *najm*
can you spot a **star**
glowing in the darkness
shining from so far?

أُوقِيَة

'uuqiyah

O is for **ounce**
My uncle shops for tea
'uuqiyah, an ounce of leaves
one for grandma, one for me.

بِطْرِيق
bittriiq

P is for **penguin**
bittriiq, aren't they sweet?
They wobble and they waddle
on those tiny webbed feet!

قِطَّة

qiṭ-ṭah

Q is for **qiṭ-ṭah**
stroke her, make her purr.
My **cat** is the perfect pet
with soft and fluffy fur.

رُمَّان

rum-maan

R is for *rum-maan*.
A **pomegranate** treat
with lemon and some sugar
it's sour and it's sweet.

SUGAR

FLOUR

BEANS

سَمَكَة

samakah

S is for **samakah**
Orange, gold and blue
A rainbow of different **fish**
hanging with their crew.

23

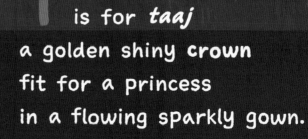

تَاج

taaj

T is for *taaj*
a golden shiny **crown**
fit for a princess
in a flowing sparkly gown.

أُذُن

'uthzun

U is for **'uthzun**
The baby grabs its **ear**
What's this funny flap of flesh?
It's what you use to hear.

sawtuk

V is for your **voice**
sawtuk, clear and loud
Tell your story, share it.
Pass it on, be proud!

26

وَرْدَة

wardah

W is for *wardah*
a **flower** for my mother
daisies are her favorite
I think I'll pick another.

X is for xylophone,
I play it while my father sings.
My aunt, *khaalah*, on tabla
Mama strums the strings.

خالة

khaalah

AA A AA
La la La

يَمَامَة

yamaamah

Y is for *yamaamah*
a gently cooing **dove**
how gracefully she's flying
and circling above.

29

Z is for **zaraafah**
A **giraffe** standing tall
its long neck stretches
towering over all.

زَرَافَة

zaraafah

بيت الزرافة

List of Words

Let's review the words we learned and their pronunciations.

Arabic Word	Pronunciation	English Word
أَهْلًا	'ahlan	welcome
بِطِّيخ	biṭ-ṭii*kh*	watermelon
سَيَّارَة	say-yaarah	car
دَرَّاجَة	dar-raajah	bike
عِيدُ الْفِطْر	'iidu-lfiṭr	Eid al-fitr
فُسْتَان	fustaan	dress
غوريلا	ghuriil-lah	gorilla
منزل	manzil	house
إِبْرَة	'ibrah	needle
جُبْن	jubn	cheese
كِتَاب	kitaab	book
لَيْمُون	laymuun	lemon
مَدْرَسَة	madrasah	school

Arabic Word	Pronunciation	English Word
نَجْم	najm	star
أُوقِيَة	'uuqiyah	ounce
بِطْرِيق	biṭṭṛiiq	penguin
قِطَّة	qiṭ-ṭah	cat
رُمَّان	rum-maan	pomegranate
سَمَكَة	samakah	fish
تَاج	taaj	crown
أُذُن	'uthzun	ear
صَوْتُك	sawtuk	voice
وَرْدَة	wardah	flower
خالة	*kh*aalah	aunt
يَمَامَة	yamaamah	dove
زَرَافَة	zaraafah	giraffe

"Books to Span the East and West"

Tuttle Publishing was founded in 1832 in the small New England town of Rutland, Vermont [USA]. Our core values remain as strong today as they were then—to publish best-in-class books which bring people together one page at a time. In 1948, we established a publishing outpost in Japan—and Tuttle is now a leader in publishing English-language books about the arts, languages and cultures of Asia. The world has become a much smaller place today and Asia's economic and cultural influence has grown. Yet the need for meaningful dialogue and information about this diverse region has never been greater. Over the past seven decades, Tuttle has published thousands of books on subjects ranging from martial arts and paper crafts to language learning and literature—and our talented authors, illustrators, designers and photographers have won many prestigious awards. We welcome you to explore the wealth of information available on Asia at www.tuttlepublishing.com.

Published by Tuttle Publishing, an imprint of
Periplus Editions (HK) Ltd.

www.tuttlepublishing.com

Text© 2023 Aya Khalil
Illustrations© 2023 Chaymaa Sobhy

Library of Congress Cataloging-in-Publication Data in process

ISBN 978-0-8048-5619-5

26 25 24 23   10 9 8 7 6 5 4 3 2 1
Printed in China   2310EP

DISTRIBUTED BY

North America, Latin America & Europe
Tuttle Publishing,
364 Innovation Drive
North Clarendon, VT 05759-9436 U.S.A.
Tel: 1 (802) 773-8930
Fax: 1 (802) 773-6993
info@tuttlepublishing.com
www.tuttlepublishing.com

Asia Pacific
Berkeley Books Pte. Ltd.
3 Kallang Sector #04-01,
Singapore 349278
Tel: (65) 6741-2178
Fax: (65) 6741-2179
inquiries@periplus.com.sg
www.tuttlepublishing.com